Fuel For Life

30 Day Devotional

Book I

By Stanford Senior, Jr.

Dedication

This devotional is dedicated to all those people in my life that have pushed me to break out of the box I became so comfortable in. They moved me when I allowed procrastination to dim my voice as they inspired me to let my gift loose and let God use it for His plan. They saw something in me worth sharing with the world.

Let's start with my parents Stanford and Monica Senior. They have been  my fuel my entire life. Of course, there are others to mention like my wife Meran Senior, Marsha Senior, Gary Sean Mullings, Cecil and Delores Mullings, Bruce Rabon, CGJPS crew, iKORT, Clifton Manning, Jr., Carlos Gonzalez, and even Lenny Pollard.

Introduction

Everything in this life needs fuel to grow or function to its maximum capability. Motor vehicles need gasoline and oil, plants need water and sun light, and humans need food and rest. In order to maximize functionality, there must be fuel. This also is a reality for every people living this life with all its ups, downs, and winding turns. Jesus reveals in Matthew 4 that, "No one can live only on food. People need every word that God has spoken." The wonderful truth is that God has always made it a priority to speak to His people concerning their everyday life and He still is speaking today.

God can be heard in everyday common circumstances and innuendos throughout our lives whether through song lyrics, movie titles, and personal conversations. With clear distinction, God speaks to us and the question is, are we really listening and perceiving His thoughts about us? This 30-Day devotional's main goal is to interject fuel for your daily life through daily inspiration to refocus your perspective on God's love, plan, and presence in your daily life. You can read this devotional in sequential order or simply chose to randomly pick a day to read based on your own situation. Hear God's voice today and allow His word to fuel your life.

-   **Stanford W. Senior, Jr**

~~SHOULD~~ ~~WOULD~~ ~~COULD~~ DID

Anonymous

Table of Contents

Whatz Good?..1

Ain't No Stopping Us Now 5

More Than Meets the Eye...9

Prison Break: No Limits...13

Access Granted..17

You Are not Alone...21

It's a Setup...25

New Day...29

The Storm is Over Now...33

Labor Day: No Breaks...37

What's in Your Hand?..41

Time to Play the Game..45

I Am Not My Hair..49

You Aren't the Only One..53

Be Blessed..57

Tripping Off His Goodness……………………..…………….61

What's Under Your Mask………………………………....65

I See You…………………………………………….69

We're Moving On Up…………………………….73

Don't Give Up…………………………….77

I'm Still Here………………………………....81

Don't Be Scared……………………………....85

I've Got The Power……………………..89

Dare To Love………………………………..93

Time for a Beat Down………………………….97

He Chose to Come to You……………………………….101

Day to Day………………………………………….105

Can't You See It?………………………………………109

Foot Prints……………………………………………….113

The FORCE be with you…………………………………117

REFERENCE PAGE………………………………….121

ABOUT THE AUTHOR……………………………….122

<u>**Whatz Good?**</u>

Whatz good? This is an interesting urban colloquialism often used as an informal way of asking how someone is doing. How often do we casually ask people that we encounter, "How are you?" without really expecting a real answer? We ask this question in passing but really never pause long enough to get an answer.

Honestly, I think this question is highly underrated both by the person asking and the person answering. Perhaps this question was meant to be a personal checkup to gauge our current condition mentally, physically, emotionally, etc… I don't want to run off the deep end but think about it. When was the last time you honestly did a personal check up to know how you were doing? God made it a priority to visit Adam and Eve in the Garden of Eden for a check on them. *"So the Lord God called out to the man, "Where are you?"* (Gen. 3:9 NIV)

We often live our lives running the rat race without checking ourselves for weaknesses, internal issues that linger, or hurt that negatively affects our decisions and tendencies. Ironically, our cars, which are designed to achieve peak performance, are also equipped with tools that constantly evaluate their condition so that you can be alerted when something is wrong. The hope is that when the check engine light comes on, you'll address the issue. This is the maintenance process of preserving the max performance of most vehicles.

Likewise, we need to have a system of evaluating ourselves so that we can address the various issues of our lives that can adversely affect how we perform or live our lives. Consider this, when someone asks you whatz good or how are you? Think about how you really are. You may not answer them with a laundry list of problems, but if thought through, you actually may discover something that needs your immediate attention. Consider it your personal check up. Take some time to do a personal check up and address any issues that you notice. My mother always told me this proverb: "Prevention is better than cure." It is better to prevent something than to have to repair it, but even better to repair it before it fails completely.

Supplemental Scriptures

1 Corinthians 11:28	Psalm 139:23	Psalm 26:2
Psalm 4:4	Lamentations 3:4	Galatians 6:4

Prayer

Lord, You know my ins and outs and all that pertains to my life. There is nothing that I can hide from You. Help me to examine myself so that I can confront any issues that arise in my life that would cause me to drift from You.. Lord, help me to see clearly so that I can be free of weights and sins that easily beset me through confession. I give you every struggle and rejoice in Your grace and liberty. I will never be the same in Jesus's name. Amen

<u>Personal Thoughts</u>

Check yourself
Sometimes you are the toxic person; sometimes you are
mean and negative
Sometimes the problem is you and that does not make
you less worthy
Keep growing; keep checking yourself
Mistakes are opportunities; look at them; own them;
grow from them
Move on; your human; it's okay

Anonymous

Ain't No Stopping Us Now

I always loved going roller skating although I was never really a great skater. I would look in amazement as more savvy looking skaters would roll around the rink with such ease and lack of fear as I simply attempted to avoid meeting my quota of multi-digit falls. The other aspect of roller skating that I always loved was the energetic music that would motivate everyone to enjoy the moment no matter how skilled or lack of skill you had. There was a popular and melodious song that everybody jammed to when the DJ would hit the volume button. As the beat dropped, every skater and those not skating would tune up, "Ain't no stopping us now! We're on the move! … Ain't no stopping us now! We've got the groove..."

This popular song released in 1979 and sung by McFadden & Whithead has been a hit in clubs and roller-skating rinks for years. Beyond the music, the song carries a theme that is universally inspiring as the definition of inner fortitude, positive thinking, and determination as you face life's hardships and struggles. Life seems to throw obstacles and roadblocks at us constantly. Sometimes those obstacles are situations; Sometimes those obstacles are people; Other times they could well be our very own failures and inner struggles.

The driving point to the song is to overcome despite the obstacles that we face. Regardless of the obstacles that you encounter, you can confront them all and overcome knowing that God is with you. *"If God be for you, who can be against you?"* (Romans 8:31 NIV) Since God is with you, Ain't no stopping you now, you're on the move. Since God is with you, put yourself back together and let nothing hold you back. Be encouraged that when you step out in assurance with the knowledge that God is with you, you can face any challenge head on in the strength that He provides.

<u>Supplemental Scriptures:</u>

Psalm 23	Jeremiah 1:19	Jeremiah 20:11
John 10:29	1 John 4:4	Romans 8:32

<u>Prayer</u>

Lord, thank you for always having my back in every struggle and obstacle. In the midst of the hardest times, You've kept me and overshadowed me from all disappointment and frustrations that cloud my mind and hinder my progress. Give me strength to keep pushing forward and rid me of negative thoughts and people who will deflate my momentum. Help me to finish strong and glorify Your great name in Jesus' name. Amen.

<u>Personal Thoughts</u>

"Courage is the most important of all the virtues because without courage, you can't practice any other virtue consistently."

Maya Angelou

More Than Meets the Eye

I grew up a heavy cartoon watcher. I can vividly remember my running home to view my hierarchy of great cartoons like Silverhawks, Duck tales, Thundercats, and Voltron among many others. One of my favorite cartoons of all times was Transformers. For those who are familiar with it, you should be well aware of its mantra…" More Than Meets the Eye". For those unaware of the backstory, let me enlighten you.

Transformers were sentient robotic lifeforms from another planet that had come to earth. The uniqueness of these robots were that they were able to blend into the society by transforming into everyday vehicles, appliances, and weapons. You would see that car driving down the street and not know that it was a robot in disguise. Hence, the mantra, "More than meets the eye." There was something more about them than what the physical eyes could see.

This surely is relatable to many people in reality. So often we seem restricted to others' appraisal of us. We find ourselves undervalued and minimized. For a moment, consider this truth for your own life. There is more to you than what I can see. God has a quite different way of seeing us than people. He told Samuel, *"People look at the outward appearance, but the Lord looks at the heart."* (1 Samuel 16:7 NIV) There is something of value about you that most people can't see. Every diamond starts from an ugly coal that is more than meets the eye and when processed, it becomes one of the most valuable substances on earth.

Let me apply the truth to you with a broad stroke. There is more value in you than has been witnessed. Don't let anyone or anything devalue your self-worth. When you look in the mirror, remind yourself that there is more to you than meets the eye. Take confidence today. There is great value in you even if no one notices. You're more interesting, significant, impressive, important, and valuable. You cannot be judged by the cover of your life. There is more to you than meets the eye.

<u>Supplemental Scripture</u>s:

1 Chronicles 28:9	Deuteronomy 32:10	Genesis 1:27
Jeremiah 29:11	Ephesians 2:4-7	Psalm 8

<u>Prayer</u>

Lord, thank you that you find me valuable.   I am grateful that You consider me valuable beyond my looks or talent. You're love for me is so great and I can't make it without You. You thought I was worth saving, keeping, and dying for. Help me to realize how valuable I am to you. Help me to see myself the way You see me and commit myself to becoming who You desire me to be. Thank you for being my mirror. I trust your evaluation of me. Let it change me forever in Jesus' name. Amen

Personal Thoughts

"Know your worth. Then add tax."

Anonymous

12

Prison Break: No Limits

Maya Angelou penned some of Black history's most eloquent and powerful poems that have inspired so many throughout her time and years afterwards. One of my favorites is "I Know Why the Caged Bird Sings". It is a powerful poem that symbolizes the value and significance of freedom.   In John 10:10, the Bible describes the agenda of the Devil in our lives. The enemy comes against us with a threefold mission: to steal, kill, and destroy. His main goal is to completely wipe you out. If that fails, he's more than satisfied to just hinder your destiny and purpose or slow your momentum by strapping you down with limitations. These limits are purposed to debilitate our progress.

Limits are restrictions and confines to which you become imprisoned and bound. He institutes limits on your mind, your finances, your education, your ministry, and your personal relationship with Christ. He will attach limits anywhere. He will do anything to frustrate your resolve. If we were only left with that to ponder, we might just give up. You cannot allow yourself to be overwhelmed by what the devil is doing because although he is active against you, Jesus is active for you. Keep reading the verse. It later describes Jesus' agenda and activity in our lives. The enemy comes to steal, kill, and destroy but according to the same scripture, Jesus comes to give us abundant life. Jesus said that he came so that you would have life and the life He gives is abundant (*overflowing*).

Everything you do and say should have life and not just any life. Life more abundantly or in another translation, "to the fullest".

Jesus wants you to live life to the fullest in Him. He enables you to break free of all that separates you from a life with Him. Break free to live life with Christ to the fullest; A life with "No Limits"

<u>Supplemental Scriptures:</u>

| 2 Corinthians 9:8 | Ephesians 3:20 | Matthew 6:33 |
| Psalm 23:5 | Romans 15:13 | Psalm 66:8-12 |

<u>Prayer</u>

Lord, thank you that You have helped me to be aware of the enemy of my soul who seeks to bind me in limitations. I thank you more that as busy as he is, you're more actively working in and on my life to bring me into Your abundance. Lord, complete Your work in me that my life might be a reflection of Your light and truth. Help me to be a mirror of You, that when people see and encounter me, they will experience Your presence and your hands on my life. Bless the works of my hands that they will testify of you and draw others to You in Jesus' name. Amen.

<u>Personal Thoughts</u>

"Live as though today is your last, love as though tomorrow will never come, and dream as if there are no limits."

Gary Westfal, <u>Dream Operative</u>

<u>**Access Granted**</u>

I am a person of routine. I have to leave my keys in a certain place every day in order to find them the next day. This translates to so much of my life. I recall one day leaving my employee badge at home because I didn't place it in the normal spot and in the morning, I was rushing to work. Of course, the badge didn't come with me. As I got to the entrance to my job, I quickly discovered how difficult the day would end up being because I would have difficulty all day accessing anything at work. I couldn't get in the office and other key areas; not even the bathroom. Everything that I needed to accomplish the demands of the job was dependent on the possession of my ID card. It was my means of access to all I needed.

Ephesians 2:18 says, "*for through him we both have access in one Spirit to the Father.*" I like to call that Access Granted! Through Jesus we have access to God and all the resources that we need to get through life successfully according to God's plan for us. He gives us free access so that we can accomplish His will and live fulfilling lives. Imagine every time you pray, God looked at you, your problem, and your needs and replied, "ACCESS GRANTED!" This would drastically change your perspective about prayer, and instantly inflate your confidence so that you would take advantage of the access God affords us, through His Son who has made a way to significantly create an access point between us and God. Consider what you would have access to.

<u>**Access Granted to more:**</u>
1. Peace in the storm
2. Grace for your weakness
3. Provision for your lack
4. Strength for your hardship
5. Power to overcome challenges
6. Mercy for your mistakes
7. Comfort for your sorrow
8. Wisdom for your decisions
9. Endurance for your trials
10. Joy for your life

Whatever you need, as much as you need, whenever you need, just go to Jesus and you'll have access to God. Through His transaction on Calvary, you have, "ACCESS GRANTED!"

<u>**Supplemental Scriptures:**</u>

| Ephesians 3:12 | John 10:7 | John 14:6 |
| Ephesians 2:20 | Ephesians 2:6 | Hebrews 10:20 |

<u>Prayer</u>

Lord, thank you that you have granted me access to your presence. You have assured me that because of the work on Calvary and the shedding of Jesus' blood that I have access innumerable resources that I need for life. Thank you for your love, your mercy, and your grace. Thank you for making a way for me to get to you. Help me to realize that you are available to me and in you, I have everything I need. Help me to always cherish my access and never to neglect it in Jesus' name. Amen

Personal Thoughts

"When God sees you doing your part, developing what
He has given you, then He will do His part and open
doors that no man can shut"

Anonymous

You Are not Alone

The late great Michael Jackson, considered the king of pop, sang a notable song entitled, "You are not alone". The song was a touching ballad and very popular. It connected with an article that I read in the Daily News. The article was based on Mother Theresa's struggle with faith before she died. This seemed strange for many because of her prominence in modern Christianity. As strange as it seems, the truth is, being a Christian doesn't prevent us from having problems and struggles. Our Christianity isn't measured by the amount of troubles we have in our lives.

When you think about it, we are not alone in our struggles. Sometimes when you find yourself struggling with faith, you feel that you are the only one dealing with that type of situation. You may feel that your circumstances are unique to you. Let me make it clear to you: You aren't.

There is someone either in the past or someone today who has gone through what you are dealing with. No struggle or issue is unique to you. The Bible says in 1 Cor. 10:13, *"No temptation has overtaken you except what is common to mankind. And God is faithful; he will not let you be tempted beyond what you can bear. But when you are tempted, he will also provide a way out so that you can endure it."* You are not alone. Jacob's alone time gave away to an encounter with God. Be encouraged that you are never alone. God makes a promise to never leave you or forsake you but even more spectacular is that He can relate to what we are feeling. Hebrews 4:15 says, *"For we do not have a high priest who is unable to empathize with our weaknesses, but we*

*have one who has been tempted in every way, just as we are—yet
he did not sin."*

Grip the reality that you truly aren't alone in whatever you are
going through. I'll end with the lyrics of a popular impactful
hymn. *Jesus knows all about our struggles. He will guide till the
day is done. There is not a friend like the lowly Jesus. No not one.
No not one.* I want you to know that you are not alone in your
struggle. Jesus is with you.

<u>Scriptural Reference</u>

1 Corinthians 10:13	Hebrews 4:15	Psalm 139:8
Matthew 11	Deuteronomy 31:8	Joshua 1:9

<u>Prayer</u>

Lord, Oftentimes I feel alone. Hear my cry and attend unto my
prayer. I am overwhelmed with life. But thank you Lord that I am
never alone. You promised to never leave or forsake me. So I
know that I am not alone in this situation because you are with me.
You will guide me through my circumstances and give me strength
for the journey. Lord, calm my nerves and embrace me in your
love till we get through this together in Jesus's name. Amen.

Personal Thoughts

"Just knowing you're not alone is often enough to kindle hope amid tragic circumstances."

Richelle E. Goodrich, <u>Smile Anyway</u>

It's a Setup

Consider Genesis 32:24. Jacob was left alone to deal with his challenges. I'm sure he felt isolated and overwhelmed with little support in the midst of uncertainty. Oftentimes, it seems that we are all alone in our struggles. It turned out that he wasn't alone because his perceived isolation was a preparation for a wrestling match with God that would eventually change the trajectory of his life. Long story short, his seeming isolation was a setup for God to reveal his destiny.

Jacob begins wrestling with God and God touches his hip, pulls it out of socket, and gives Jacob a limp. This seems so unfair but in actuality, God was wrestling destiny out of Jacob. His limp was a breaking point in the match. His limp signified that God was moving in his life and sometimes God allows you to experience a breaking. This isn't the end but a setup for greater things to be accomplished in your life.

Jacob's wrestling became holding on for what God would eventually do in His life. He declared, "I will not let you go until you bless me." We need to have this same resolve in our lives today. Stop fighting God and instead hold on to Him until He completes His work in your life and releases His best. God seeing Jacob's persistence, asked Jacob, "What's your name?" He eventually changed his name from Jacob to Israel signifying a change in identity and a change in trajectory.

God had setup the whole encounter in order to bless Jacob. He knew everything about Jacob's story; He knew his past and his weaknesses yet He still planned to bless His life. Today, God is setting you up for a blessing but it includes a breaking that cannot be avoided. Keep trusting that He will bring you out because He will. Keep holding onto Him because your persistence will produce His revelation, His purpose, and the fulfillment of His promise. It's all a setup.

<u>Supplemental Scriptures:</u>

Psalm 17:5	Psalm 121:3	Psalm 119:133
1 Samuel 2:9	Psalm 40:2	Proverbs 4:26

<u>Prayer</u>

Lord, thank you that you have intentionally set me up to bless me. Often our encounters seem to hurt me but you have a plan in store to make me better. Lord, help me to endure your breaking that I can enjoy your blessings. Take out of me everything that draws me away from my greater purpose. I yield my life to you because you know what's best for me. Change my mind and my life so that it moves in sync with your plans. Thank you that you are leading me into my best days. Continue to work on me till you're finished with your masterpiece in Jesus' name. Amen.

Personal Thoughts

"That difficulty isn't meant to defeat you; Its meant to promote you. A setback is simply a setup for a greater comeback"

Joel Osteen

<u>**New Day**</u>

Christianity has been the best thing that has happened in my life. I'll start this conversation with that point and let it marinate. As much as I love and appreciate this God relationship that has consumed my existence, it didn't come with a disclaimer. Yes, the owner's manual explains the ins and outs with great descriptive instructions and examples but no one really thoroughly explained that this journey is would not be an easy one. Maybe I am just the only naïve person who mistakenly assumed this wonderful relationship would be a bed of roses. Now make no mistake, God has been great. It's just been various people and assorted circumstances that have created these "valley" moments.

These moments when you begin to question your faith, your purpose, and your own existence. These moments when prayer seems fruitless and there are more questions and complaints than viable answers. Can you relate? In these moments, God seems so far away and you feel too tired, frustrated, or overwhelmed to make an attempt to find Him. Can you relate? These moments push you to the limit and you feel the intensity of the midnight and just wished that the day would end. Can you relate?

David knew this moment that I speak about. He captured his moment in Psalm 23:4, *"Even though I walk through the darkest valley, I will fear no evil, for you are with me;"* David felt the grips of life's weights that easily overwhelm us and it ushered him into a valley. He described it as a shadow of death. Have you ever felt overwhelmed by the shadow of death? The great thing about this terrible experience was that God was with him and the experience eventually gave way to a new day.

David further captured this thought in Psalm 30:5. There he says, *"weeping may stay for the night, but rejoicing comes in the morning."* Wow! The long dreary midnight must give way to a morning or in this case a NEW DAY! God has a new day on the horizon of your circumstance but you have to choose to not allow the lingering pain of your night experience extinguish your hope of the materialization of God's shift on your behalf. Just hold on for in a moment, your night will end and you will have a new day. A "New Day" is practically another chance to live and enjoy life. It's another day and opportunity to call someone and tell them "I love you". It's another chance to make things right and say "I'm sorry". Today, take advantage of your new day.

Supplemental Scriptures:

Psalm 30:5	Psalm 143:8	Psalm 59:16
Lamentations 3:22-23	Luke 1:78-80	Psalm 118:24

Prayer

Lord, I am grateful that you are a faithful God that is always concerned about me. I know that my situation is painful and overwhelming, but you've have promised that it is seasonal. Your word says that weeping only endures for the night, but joy comes in the morning. Thank you Lord for giving me a "morning" in my situation so that I may experience a change. I will make it because you have a new day in store for me. Thank you Lord for another chance to get it right with you and others. Thank you Lord for my new day in Jesus name. Amen.

Personal Thoughts

"Write it on your heart
that every day is the best day in the year.
He is rich who owns the day, and no one owns the day
who allows it to be invaded with fret and anxiety."

Ralph Waldo Emerson, <u>Collected Poems and
Translations</u>

The Storm is Over Now

I love Kirk Franklin. His ministry has been a blessing to my
Christian walk ever since the first CD that I purchased as a new
Christian. There is one particular song that he penned that is so
encouraging. "It's Over Now" This song resonated in my mind as
I reflected on the yearly outlook of terrifying hurricanes and
inclement weather that often terrorize the world with climate
change including torrential rain and boisterous winds that create
havoc in small islands and coastlands. These storms have been
historically menacing damaging property, economies, and even
claiming enumerable amounts of human life.

I've come to realize that we all face storms from time to time.
These storms in our lives can swiftly appear without warning and
just as quick as they arrive, they can decimate our routines and our
comfort. These storms aren't always about rain and wind speed.
Sometimes our storms are emotional, financial, physical, or even
spiritual. These storms can attack our marriage, our family life,
our financial stability, our career aspirations, or our spiritual
connections. Our storms aren't always the same length or
intensity. They can last for day or extend for years.

Storms are inescapable. The question is not if you will experience
a storm but when. You are reading this and you either have come
through a storm, you are currently in one, or there is one that you
will encounter eventually. Storms are terrifying. They destroy
anything in their path with no respect of person. A great truth to
always remember when you find yourself in a storm is that God is
a storm shifter. He has power over the winds and the waves. The

disciples marveled at Jesus' ability to speak to the winds and the waves and they obeyed His commands like children acquiescing to their parent's orders. No matter what storm is that you are facing, know that God is in the storm with you and He can cause the storm to shift or cease. God can give your storm a cease and desist order and that Hurricane tormenting you will either have to move or end. Begin to acknowledge God in prayer and watch God shift your storm. Be encouraged by Psalm 107:29-30 NIV. "*He stilled the storm to a whisper; the waves of the sea[a] were hushed.*" Don't worry or fret because the storm is over now. You can make it through this.

Supplemental Scriptures:

Psalm 65:7	Psalm 89:9	Matthew 8:26
Mark 4:39	Mark 4:41	Luke 8:24

Prayer

Lord, I am in a storm. I feel like I'm drowning. Lord, I need your help. I look to you to come to my rescue. Save me from the downpours in my life. Save me from the winds and the waves. Be the captain and help me to get out of this storm safely. My ship is rocking but I depend on you to anchor me. Thank you that you have power over the winds and the waves. Thank you for being my lighthouse to lead me to safety in Jesus' name, Amen.

Personal Thoughts

"Don't pray for an easy life. Pray for the strength to
endure a difficult one"

Bruce Lee

Labor Day: No Breaks

Labor Day is a national US holiday celebrated on the first Monday in September. It honors the American Labor Movement and the impact of laborers on the society. It is a day that celebrates labor. From early on in human history, people have had to work and labor in life. The Bible is filled with admonishment for those who labor and rebukes people who are lazy. I remember my first job was a janitor at my high school during the summer break. It was a fun job that paid well considering that I was my first job and my first experience in the workforce. As fun getting paid was, they worked us extensively. Understand that it was a summer job during the dog days of summer with daily rise in the heat index and moments where I wanted to go home.

 Thinking about this makes me appreciate labor laws that mandate that workers get specified lunch breaks as well as other breaks during their work schedule. As much as I loved payday, I also loved getting a break during work where I could get a temporary interruption to the work load. Every employer is legally bound to give their employees break times. I don't think that I ever ignored taking my break time. I mean, since I had to by law. (wink, wink)

On a greater level, when I consider Jesus, the greatest worker of all time, His resume is impressive. He made the Heavens and the earth with the power of His words. He created every living thing and has orchestrated the preservation of life. He came to earth to live a perfect life and died a sinner's death miraculously resurrecting from the grave. Jesus then rose from the grave, ascended back to Heaven and currently right now continually intercedes on our behalf daily. The beautiful thing is that He diligently works without taking breaks. He works 24 hours, 7 days, 365 days of the year. Every day of your life, Jesus puts on his hard hat and goes to work for your good. He doesn't request a break; He doesn't file grievances about His work conditions. He works so that you will experience God's "good" ... Romans 8:28 (NIV) says, "*And we know that in all things God works for the good of those who love him, who have been called according to his purpose.*" All things work together because Jesus is putting in the work. Pause awhile and thank God for His great work in your life. Please be patient. God is not through working on you yet.

Supplemental Scriptures:

Philippians 2:12-13	Isaiah 26:12	Jeremiah 31:33
Acts 11:21	Hebrews 13:21	Titus 3:4-5

Prayer

Lord, how can I thank you for all that you have done in my life? You are always making a way for me. By your power and might, you have lifted me up from sin and sorrow. You have worked a great work in my life. Mighty are the works of your hands. Help me to remember all that you do day to day to secure me and bless me. Receive my praise and an offering of thanksgiving for who you are but also for what you have done, is doing, and shall do in Jesus' name. Amen.

Personal Thoughts

"No Human masterpiece has been created with great labor"

Andre Gide

What's in Your Hand?

Driving to work this morning, I saw the hustle and bustle of students heading into school to face new challenges and new expectations. Truth is, we all go through this whether you're a student, parent, spouse, etc... Every day seems to present to us some new challenge. Some of them we were expecting but many times, these unexpected challenges leave us perplexed and frustrated.

Life always presents new challenges and expectations that often times are heaped on you from day to day. Whether it is trying to find a babysitter or perhaps attempting to complete a project before the due date, challenges and expectations will always arise on the job, in the marriage, or even in the pews of the church. In Exodus 3 & 4, Moses is given a task that presents him with a new challenge along with great expectation and like most of us, he wondered how he would succeed under the pressure.

In chapter 4:2, God asks Moses a paramount question similar to what He is asking you today. "*What's that in your hand*?" God is not asking you this to gain some knowledge about you. He is God and He already knows. He uses the question as a means of revelation to us. He wants us to answer the question and simultaneously come to grips with what He is revealing in us. So, answer the question. What is that in your hand? I know your problem or issue is on your mind, but take a minute and ponder the question.

In other words, God is revealing that what you need to succeed is already in your hands. "You already Got it!". That's not proper English but it expresses the point. You already got it? You have what you need to solve that problem. God has graced you with what you need. You are already equipped to succeed in this challenge. Just go out there and face those challenges and win because you got what it takes to succeed.

Supplemental Scriptures:

Jeremiah 1:5-6	Romans 12	1 Corinthians 12
1 Peter 4	Ephesians 4	1 Corinthians 14:1

Prayer

Lord, you are a great God who plans great things for your people. You give us purpose which oftentimes overwhelms us because you ask us to do things beyond our capability. You told Noah to build an ark; You told Moses to confront a tyrant. You told the disciples to evangelize the world. Thank you for trusting us with gifts and talents but I need your grace to see what you see in me. Thank you that you have given me the resources to be great. Help me to always depend on you as I activate what you have placed in me. Always get the glory and honor; always go with me so that I may be victorious in Jesus' name. Amen.

"Your future is in your hand, now go and create it"

Anonymous

<u>Time to Play the Game</u>

I love wrestling. Not the high school or Olympic wrestling. That sports is cool but I'm more interested in the jumping off the top rope, smack talking, drop kicking type of wrestling. Yes, its scripted, but in my opinion it is real action. I grew up watching WWF, now WWE, and I love the action, the fighting, and the music. In 1995 I discovered a young cocky wrestling character and in ring performer named Triple H. His charismatic and daring persona made him an instant hit as he proclaimed his superiority among all other competitors. As his career developed, he proved many of his claims as he rose to the pinnacle of the sport. Later he would adopt an epic theme song for his ring entrance. The song loudly rang out in the arena and through the television, "It's Time to Play the Game..!"

This sounds funny just reciting it but it also has deep meaning though. Often in life we sit on the sidelines and complain about our situation instead of doing something about it. We become immobile and perched in a stationary position. We complain more than strategizing. We complain and ultimately rehearse our excuses for our circumstances. We'll even complain and declare to the world that we are waiting for God to do something when in truth, God is waiting on us to do something. Psalm 1 says, "whatsoever he doeth shall prosper". The key word is doeth. You have got to do something. No wonder Nike claimed the mantra, "Just Do it!"

You cannot sit still any longer and expect that anything is going to change on its own. God declared to Israel that He had given the

Promise Land to them but they had to go and fight and take it in order to fulfill the promise. It is our responsibility to move into action at some point. Yes, pray, but do something. Trust God, but do something. Have faith, but you must also realize when it's time to play the game and activate that faith. How about studying if you are failing a course? How about saving and cut some spending if you want to change your finances? God promises to direct your path when you acknowledge him, so trust Him that He will give you victory when you get in the game.

Supplemental Scriptures:

James 1:22	1 Corinthians 16:13	Luke 12:35
Revelation 3:2	Ephesians 5:16	Ecclesiastes 9:10

Prayer

Lord, I have been a prisoner to procrastination for way too long. I have allowed my gifts get stagnant as I have wasted precious opportunities to advance your Kingdom or establish your purpose in my life. Lord, help me to get up out of complacency and mediocrity. Help me to move in sync with you. Bless the works of my hands as I follow the Psalm 1 blessing. I know that you are going to bless me so I give you praise in advance. Move on my behalf in Jesus' name. Amen.

Personal Thoughts

"Get in the game. Do the best you can. Try to make a contribution. Learn from today. Apply it to tomorrow"

Cal Ripken, Jr.

I Am Not My Hair

One day as I was walking towards work, I noticed a big bold red banner on the side of a bus. I can't remember what message was on the banner but I clearly remember how the banner stood out and distracted me from anything else on the side of the bus. This caused me to think of the many labels in the world that grab our attention but come up short of telling the whole story. Labels become our way of defining things or people. We are surrounded by labels; big ones and little ones; dull ones and bright ones. Wherever you are in this country, there is someone practically slapping a label on you in an attempt to define you, your company, your culture, your situation, or even your future. Labels are on everything and even people. We label people all the time and oftentimes we do it subconsciously. We use our labels to define them and often place them in all sorts of categories and we often come up short of telling the person's whole story. Most of our labels are wrong.

Think of some that you may have heard. You are too: small, big, tall, smart, prude, dark, just to mention a few. India Arie had a great point when she sang her hit, "I am not my hair". She clearly emphasizes the importance of not judging people according to the labels we view them with. I can hear the inference. Don't judge me according to your limited perspective or opinion of me. The old adage stands true. "Don't judge a book by its cover." You might just miss out on a treasure or you might invest in a dud.

This world is so diverse with its cultures, nations, and people. Each one bringing value and distinctiveness to the conversation.

Such diversity is both beautiful and mysterious. We can't afford to prejudge people by their distinction and what makes us different. We shouldn't label or attempt to define people by superficial things.   We should be defined by who God says we are. God looks at us beyond the label that people place on us. Here are a few descriptions God says about you that you should consider: royal, loved, forgiven, protected, favored, blessed, chosen, precious, purposed, healed, delivered, mighty, wonderful, victorious, and the greatest of all, HIS. Remember, when people want to label you, that you are not your hair. You are who and what God says you are.

<u>Supplemental Scriptures:</u>

Matthew 7:1-2	Acts 4:13	2 Corinthians 5:17
James 2:1-7	Galatians 3:27-29	Isaiah 45:17

<u>Prayer</u>

Heavenly Father, thank you that you don't see me the way people do.   Thank you that you don't measure my worth based on my past mistakes or the labels that people usually use to describe me. You love with me with an everlasting love and continually pursue me for a relationship. Lord, you see me as valuable. You look beyond my faults and see my needs. Thank you for loving me in spite of me and always leading me to my best life. Help me to not succumb to the labels that people want to place on me. Help me to live up to your standard and desire for my life in Jesus' name. Amen.

Personal Thoughts

"I am not my hair. I am not my skin. I am the soul that lives within"

Indie Arie

<u>**You Aren't the Only One**</u>

There was a game show called Temptation. It was a new show with the same old gimmicks. The gist of this show was that contestants were offered fabulous prizes at the cost of the money that they have already gained in previous rounds of the show. The contestants could either ignore the temptation and continue their progress or give up what they had gain for a chance at some perceived pleasure.

Doesn't this sound similar to Joseph's story in Genesis? Every day Joseph would go to work and become a target of Potiphar's wife's sexual solicitations. Every day he had to make a choice whether to yield or to run. Doesn't this also sound like every day for us as well? Every day we are offered some type of temptation at the cost of our progress in Christ and our relationship with God. Sadly enough, sometimes we yield and find out on the back end that the seemingly pleasurable offer wasn't even worth the time, energy, and heartache. The Bible says in 1 Cor. 10:13 that the temptations that come in your life are no different from what others experience. You experience the same temptation that your mother, father, grandmother or grandfather experienced. Actually, you experience the same temptation that the people around you experience. Can I make it even more relevant and personal? Jesus, Himself, and the people of the Bible experienced the same temptations that you do. In other words, you aren't the only one. Sometimes we feel that we are the only ones in the midst of a temptation. This is a ploy of the enemy as he plays on our vulnerability in hopes of separating us from our strength; our connections. But the truth is, you aren't the only one dealing with it and the Bible says that it is common to man.

Here is the gem to treasure. When you are tempted, God will show you a way out so that you can escape it. Whatever the temptation, no matter how enticing, you aren't the only one going through it and you aren't alone to deal with it because God is standing beside you to guide you through it. Always remember that it isn't a sin to be tempted but a sin to yield. Yielding isn't the only option. God will make a way of escape. Try looking away from the temptation but look and see God trying to navigate you through it. There is a way of escape or better yet, an alternative route that God is trying to point you to. Choose wisely.

<u>Supplemental Scriptures:</u>

Luke 22:46	Hebrews 11:37	James 5:10
Revelation 2:10	Psalm 89:33	2 Thessalonians 3:3

<u>Prayer</u>

Heavenly Father, I am so glad that you are my God. If you left to myself, I would surely ruin all that you have established in my life. I am grateful that in every temptation that I feel, I am not the only one experiencing it and that you have already made a way of me escaping the trap. Without you I would fail, so please Lord, give me grace to always choose you. Give me grace to always choose the higher road that you might be honored in my decisions. Guide through all wilderness experiences. Help me avoid every pitfall set up against me. May the words of my mouth and the meditation of my heart be acceptable in your sight. My strength and my Redeemer in Jesus/ name. Amen.

<u>Personal Thoughts</u>

Everyone goes through a hard time in their life"

Kristen Dunst

Be Blessed

I was listening to a Yolanda Adam's song named "Be Blessed" and it really grabbed my attention. As much as the song blessed me, it also challenged my perspective of God's blessings and the responsibility of being a conduit of His blessings to other people. It's so natural to desire to be blessed and please understand that there is nothing wrong with that. In 1 Chronicles 4:10 (NIV), Jabez prayed, "*O that thou would bless me and enlarge my territory...*" I do believe that we should seek God's assistance in every aspect of our lives. He desires for us to receive his blessings for our lives. But there must be more to life than just being a container that stores God's blessings.

Think about this. Does God really want me to selfishly horde His best? He didn't withhold giving up His only begotten Son. Why would He desire me to be so selfish? I know that you have prayed constantly for your well-being but have you ever taken time to solicit God for others? Have you ever considered speaking God's blessings over someone else's life? We casually say to someone who sneezes, "God bless you", but how many times did you mean that as genuine prayer or proclamation? How many times have you made your devotional time with God centered on other people other than yourself? It is easy to want to keep God all to yourself. The disciples once angrily reported to Jesus about others who were doing miracles in His name and how they told them to stop. Jesus quickly corrected their thinking.

You are blessed to be a blessing. God has given you His grace and the activity of His hands but He doesn't expect you to keep it to yourself but rather to share the wealth with others. I challenge you to make a proclamation of God's word and His blessings over the people you speak with this week. As much as you can remember, end each conversation, whether by phone, text or email, with this prayer: "Be Blessed!" As you seek the needs of others, watch God see about yours.

<u>Supplemental Scriptures:</u>

Mark 9:38-39	Matthew 5	Matthew 11:6
Matthew 16:7	Matthew 24:6	Luke 6

<u>Prayer</u>

Lord, you blessed my life. You have given me power to speak to situations and circumstances beyond my ability to handle. Since you have given me power in my tongue, I use it to speak blessings on my family members. I speak over my children. I speak blessings over my marriage. I speak blessings over my co-workers and classmates. Bless them in their going out and in their coming in. Blessed their finances. Blessed their dreams. Bless their prospects. Bless their job and career. Give them favor to excel and increase in every good thing. Honor this prayer of blessing for others in Jesus' name. Amen.

Personal Thoughts

"We've been blessed so that we can bless somebody else"

Charles Hooks

<u>Tripping Off His Goodness</u>

One Saturday night I went to a coffee house at Christ's Church in Montclair, NJ. There were about two hundred and fifty other people there. It was definitely a night to remember. It was an open mic event where talent from all over the Tri-State came to share their gifts and lift up Jesus. The atmosphere was light and there was freedom of expression from a diversity of backgrounds, cultures, and experiences. Among the gifted artists that performed that evening, there was a young lady who sang this song, "Trippin off Ya Goodness". I played that song non-stop for days on end. Beyond the hypnotic and melodic vibe of the track, the message of the song was even more profound. The words drew our attention to God's goodness and the immense thought of how consistently good He is.

In Psalms 23 (NIV), David says, *" Surely your goodness and love will follow me all the days of my life…"* Goodness can be understood as God's care & provision for your life. Consider that God has assigned His goodness to follow you every day. His goodness follows you to class, on your job, in the supermarket checkout line, and everywhere else you go. Think about it. God's goodness is assigned over your every step. No wonder the Bible says in Romans 8, *"…all things work together for your good*". I have God's goodness riding shot gun with me every time I turn the key. Even when unforeseen and horrible things happen, God's goodness is somewhere near working for me. Simply incredible!

There are 3 things that I want you to contemplate about God's goodness.

        1. It reaches into every aspect of your life.
        2. It is undeserved and you can't earn it.
        3. It is the byproduct of God's love for you.

This is definitely something that will trip you up. So, the next time you realize His goodness is operating in your life, pause long enough to look to heaven and say thank you Lord for Your goodness.

Supplemental Scriptures:

Romans 8	Psalm 34:10&12	Psalm 45:1
1 Chronicles 16:25	Psalm 145:3	Psalm 48:1

Prayer

Lord, you are good and your mercy endures forever. Every time I turn around you keep blessing e. Every time that I think about all that you have done for me, I have to praise your name. Morning by morning, I receive new mercy and day by day, I am the receive your grace. Thank you Lord for being so good to me. Let me shine your goodness towards others and may the world come to know you as good. Use my life as your canvas and I will tell of your goodness always. Help me to be like you to share your goodness with those I come into contact with in Jesus' name. Amen.

Personal Thoughts

"God is so great that he can become small. God is so powerful that he can make himself vulnerable and come to us as a defenseless child, so that we can love him."

Pope Benedict XVI

<u>**What's Under Your Mask?**</u>

Every year around Halloween, I am perplexed and I scratch or shake my head as I watch grown adult people come to the work place dressed up in Halloween costumes. Yes, I said it; grown adult people spending their hard-earned money on costumes to come to work. I digress. This goes beyond whether or not I celebrate Halloween. To be clear, I don't because Halloween in stands opposed to basic biblical principles and Christian thought. It's not hard to really understand why children desire to celebrate by dressing up as their favorite superhero or athlete, but it's a whole other issue all together to watch adults doing the same thing with equal passion.

Think about it though. It is really no different every week in church, at home, or even at work for many people. Many of us walk around dressed up in a mask of Christianity.   On the surface, we look like Christians; we might sound like Christians; but often, when you peel away the religious layers, we don't live like Christians and it is obvious to most people that we encounter.

We wear the gold cross and sing all of the popular songs, but how much of it is a ritual rather than being a lifestyle? It reminds me of a group of pretenders in the book of Acts who attempted to cast out demons only to discover that it took more than an appearance to get results. Acts 19:15 describes the demon's response to these imposters. *"Jesus, I know, and Paul, I know, but who are you?"* They needed a connection to Jesus and real power to get their desired results. It was proven better to be disciples who had a bona fide relationship with Christ than to depend on the mere appearance of being a disciple.

Are you wearing a mask today? Many of us do daily. The world needs genuine Christians not just an appearance of one. The reason why so many people avoid attending church is the lack of genuine people. Let's take the mask off and stop pretending that we are these perfect people that God loves to brag on. Truth is, we make a lot of mistakes and are recipients of His great mercy, grace, and unchanging love. His love never changes and He us loves in spite of our failures. Ask yourself, "is what's underneath my mask inviting people to God or driving them away?" Take off the mask and try being genuine about who you are and your story. His grace will shine through.

<u>Supplemental Scriptures:</u>

Acts 9:15	Proverbs 15:17	1 Peter 3:3-4
Romans 12:2	Ephesians 2:10	1 Peter 5:6

<u>Prayer</u>

Lord, thank you for your compassion towards me even when I hide beneath a mask. There are so many times I hide my mistakes and sinful tendencies from people but I can't hide them from you. You see past my mask and know the intents and condition of my heart. Lord, lift the burden to prove myself to people from me and help me to be honest with myself about my habits and conditions so that I can run to you and get help. Lord, embrace me in your love and help me to stand in Jesus' name. Amen

Personal Thoughts

"You wear a mask so long; you forget who you were beneath it"

Alan Moore

<u>**I See You**</u>

While visiting someone in the hospital, I reflected on the
significance of the ICU. For many people, the thought of the ICU
brings up a lot of stress and anxiety because it generally means that
someone is so severely injured and/or sick, that they need special
attention. For the most part, I don't know anyone who would
intentionally check into the ICU for a recreational visit. I'm sure
that they would much rather head over to Disney and ride one of
the roller coasters or experience one of the famous attractions.

In God, ICU's true meaning (Intensive Care Unit) takes its fullest
and richest implication. Like the hospital's ICU, God gives
Intensive Care over every need and every hurt. Psalms 8:4 (NIV)
says, *"What is mankind that you are mindful of them, human
beings that you care for them?"* God is a loving God who is
patient to watch your moment by moment condition and
administer the necessary combination of love, mercy and grace to
cure any ailment. He has the patience to diagnose the issue,
conduct the surgery, and then nurse you through recovery. He has
the ability to give specialized treatment regardless of how many
patients He has. There is no need to stress whether or not you
have adequate coverage because at Calvary, He already paid the
full cost of your care.

The beautiful truth is, unlike a trip to the hospital's ICU, with God,
you don't need to be sick to get this treatment and there is no need
for a referral. The only requirement is faith and a trust in Him that
will allow you to give Him the case. He longs to bless you if you
wait on Him. He is the doctor, the receptionist, the nurse, and the

social worker. He handles the entire process to ensure your full recovery. This sounds like the greatest insurance plan known to man. Take a moment and rejoice at the fact that God has you in His ICU. (I See You) and He is sure to handle any case you bring to him.

<u>Supplemental Scriptures:</u>

Isaiah 39:5	Philippians 4:6-7	Hebrews 13:8
John 3:16	2 Corinthians 12:9	Psalm 55:22

<u>Prayer</u>

Lord, thank you that you are so mindful of me. You're concerned about every need. You care about every condition. There is nothing about my life that is insignificant to you. You've numbered every hair on my so I am confident that you are concerned about the integral parts of my existence. I give you my weaknesses, my tendencies, and all the areas of my life that need your attention. Heal my wounds and help me recovery wholeness in Jesus' name. Amen.

<u>Personal Thoughts</u>

"Once we surrender our mind to God completely, He will take care of us in everyway"

Sri Sathya Sai Baba

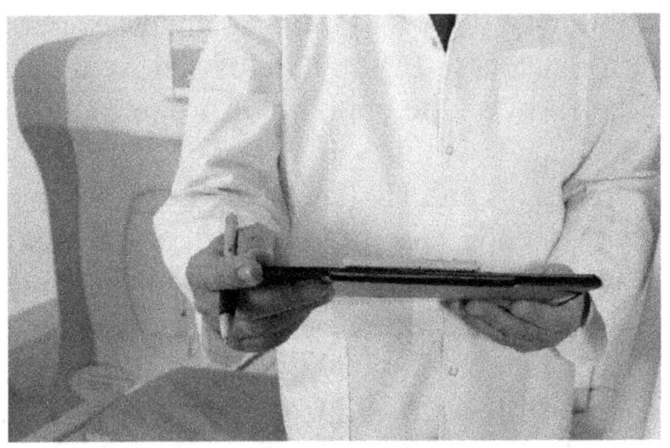

<u>**We're Moving on Up**</u>

One of my favorite shows in the 80's was the Jeffersons. If you are unfamiliar with it, it was an American sitcom that lasted approximately lasted for 11 seasons. The storyline revolves around the Jefferson family that moved from a working-class section of Queens, New York, into the luxurious Colby East high-rise apartment complex in Manhattan, NY. The show followed the daily struggles and episodes of a family on the rise and climbing the social ladder of success. If you had to surmise the show, you could describe the show as the epitome of progress.

God is a God of progress and He has created and positioned us for progress. He never intended for us to exist in a perpetual state of stagnation. We aren't designed to remain the unchanged or satisfied with mediocre but, like the Jeffersons, step by step, we are to elevate to a higher level of living physically, emotionally and spiritually. The Bible says in 2 Cor. 3:18 that we," *...are changed into the same image from glory to glory, even as by the Spirit of the Lord*." We are steadily becoming more like the only perfect person to exist: Jesus Christ, our model of holy living. We are all in a process of change leading us to a higher level in God and this process of progression includes our strengths and weaknesses; our pain and suffering; our ups and downs; our successes and our failures. From early childhood we have been on this journey and our development is in our own hands.

There are 3 things that you can use to help your progression.
1. When hardship, in any fashion, stretches you, learn to stretch out in God's grace. You won't break.
2. Learn the lessons from other people's mistakes. You don't have to fall in the pit too. Experience is not the greatest teacher.
3. Don't waste the investment. God is consistently investing resources in your life from people to unexpected opportunities. Make use of them all.

You will be perfected. You are God's masterpiece and He is steadily crafting your life. Don't allow anything to persuade you to get off His wheel until He is finished. Keep on progressing toward the higher calling of God on your life and then you can gladly proclaim, "We're moving on up!"

<u>Supplemental Scriptures:</u>

Ephesians 2:10   Psalm 100:3   Psalm 138:8
1 Corinthians 3:9   Philippians 1:6   Philippians
2:13

<u>Prayer</u>

Lord, thank you for setting my life to progress and develop. I have great expectations of what you are going to do in my present and in my future. I am convinced that you are up to something great and its going to be BIG! Thank you for letting me be a part of your bigger plan. Help me to align myself with you so that I can reap a harvest that will affect my life, my home, my family, my friends, my church and my future in Jesus' name. Amen.

Personal Thoughts

"Without continual growth and progress, such words as improvement, achievement, and success have no meaning"

Benjamin Franklin

Don't Give Up

I can vividly remember the death of Grandma Denny. She was an elderly church mother that was so impactful to so many youth and others in the church. Although she wasn't my by birth grandmother, she became a spiritual grandma for both me and others as she invested her wisdom and presence in our lives. Unfortunately for us, God decided that her time on earth had ended because He wanted her to help the stars shine.

As I recall my last conversation with her in the hospital, it tremendously moved me although she couldn't really speak to me. As her weak frail body laid there on the hospital bed, she somehow found enough strength to utter 3 words that will stay with me forever. Could it possibly be that she knew that her time was drawing to an end and she wanted to leave a deposit in me? I believe so. Out of everything she possibly could have said, she repeatedly uttered to me, "Don't Give Up!" "Don't Give Up!" "Don't Give Up!" That went through my mind over and over again. "Don't Give Up!"

What a phenomenal encouragement to grasp through the timeworn raspy voice of a grandmother of the faith: "Don't Give Up!" When you feel like your marriage is crumbling, Don't Give Up. When the bad reports of your children pile up and you feel at your wits end, Don't Give Up. When you want to leave the church for good reason, Don't Give Up. If you failed at something and the burden of discouragement is weighing you down, Don't Give Up.

You can't give up because God hasn't given up on bringing you into your best days. You can't give up because there is light at the end of the tunnel. You can't give up because God has purposed this experience to make you stronger, wiser, better. Philippians 1:6 says, "*...He that began the good work in you, will continue His work until it is finally finished...*" (NLT) Don't give up because God isn't finished working on your behalf. Let these 3 words resonate in your heart in the face of every conflict and struggle. DON'T GIVE UP!

Supplemental Scriptures:
2 Chronicles 15:7   Isaiah 41:10   Jeremiah 29:11
Galatians 6:9   Joshua 1:9   Hebrews 12:1-3

Prayer

Lord, life is tough sometimes. It rains then it pours and then rains again. There seems to be a perpetual dark cloud that I can't escape. I'm losing hope in friends and family. I've started questioning everything and everyone. If I'm honest, I sometimes question you. Lord, help me in this time of pressure, frustration and anxiety. Help me to lean on you for support because you are well able. Help me to cast these fears and weights on you so that I can walk in freedom. As I go through this season, help me to feel you near me so that I can hold on till my change comes. I place my hope in you knowing that you will get me out. Give me strength and help me to hold on till you bless me in Jesus' name. Amen.

Personal Thoughts

"Winners never quit, and quitters never win"

Vince Lombardi

I'm Still Here

One cold damp morning as I was walking towards my office, I noticed something peculiar that caught my attention. Besides the fact that the start of my day was filled with rainy inclement weather, there was a thick cloud of fog blocking and covering my building. The cloud seemed like something out of a movie and the visibility was so low that I could no longer see where my building was. Beyond seeming very creepy, this got me thinking about the many times my view of God is blocked by a fog of life's circumstances. Oftentimes in life we can't see, hear or feel God either because our sin, issues or perhaps we have allowed people to block our view of Him. As we stagger through the fog, we are left to wonder if He is even still there.

Job says in Job 23:8-9 (NLT), "*I go east, but he is not there. I go west, but I cannot find him I do not see him in the north, for he is hidden. I look to the south, but he is concealed.*" This could as well be your reality now. It is common for us to expect sunshine all everyday as we travel through life but we must also be prepared for days filled with dense thick fog that renders our path indiscernible. As I walked closer to the building in amazement of the fog, I realized that, although I couldn't see the building, it was still there. Likewise, in the midst of life's fog encumbering our focus and our stride, be encouraged that God answers back through the mist, "I'M STILL HERE!"

Understand that He hasn't left you; He hasn't abandoned you; He hasn't forgotten about you. Most times you have to ignore the distraction, hear His voice, and move towards Him. Eventually,

He will cause the fog to cease from hindering your vision. He will reveal Himself as faithful and committed to you in your greatest times of need. Keep moving towards Him and you'll find out that He was always right there. He is a faithful God and remains closer than we imagine. He truly is still there.

<u>Supplemental Scriptures:</u>

Psalm 10:1	Psalm 13:3	Proverbs 18:24
Psalm 16:8	Psalm 73:28	Psalm 34:18

<h2 style="text-align:center"><u>Prayer</u></h2>

Lord, thank you for your sustaining power. You've have preserved my life, my gifts, my purpose, my ministry, and my hope in you. You have always been there for me even when I couldn't sense you. I know that you have never left me and will always have my back. Thank you that you allow your presence to bring me peace. Let me see your glory and help me to trust your plan in Jesus' name. Amen.

Personal Thoughts

"Man's faith may fail him sometimes, but God's faithfulness never fails Him"

William Greenhill

<u>**Don't Be Scared**</u>

Of a truth, God knows how to give great gifts. Think about some for a moment. We all can attest to God's gracious provisions throughout our lives. Let's narrow in for the next 4 days on some things that God gives us based on 2 Timothy 1:7

2 Tim. 1-7 says "*God hasn't given us a spirit of fear and timidity but of power, love, and self-discipline. *" (NLT)

Don't be Scared!

Another way of appreciating what God gives us is to examine what He keeps from us. There are so many things that God doesn't allow us to deal with simply because He is good. Of the many things that God does give you, He has not given you fear. Fear intimidates you; fear imprisons you; fear will cause you to act out of character. Fear will cause you to under achieve and self-sabotage. One person defined fear as:

False Evidence Appearing Real

Fear is not a gift from God but actually a weapon of the enemy to hinder you from maximizing God given opportunities; It deters you from maximizing your gifts and talents; It will cause premature death emotionally and psychology. Matthew 14:30 illustrates the power of fear and how it held Peter back from defying the impossibility of walking on water.

The only way to handle your fears is to:
1. Acknowledge them. They are real.
2. Investigate them. Why are you feeling this way? What is the cause?
3. Face them and overcome them by faith. You can do it.

The beautiful truth is since fear doesn't originate from God, there is no reason that I need to accept it in my life. Treat fear like the email that you know has a virus that will corrupt your computer system. Don't ignore it and definitely don't open it. Immediately send it to the trash. It doesn't belong in your system.

<u>Supplemental Scriptures:</u>

Acts 20:24	Romans 8:15	Acts 21:13
Hebrews 2:15	1 john 4:18	Matthew 6:34

<u>Prayer</u>

Lord, you haven't given me fear. I have no reason to fear because you are my light and my salvation. There is no goliath or mountain that is bigger than you. You are greater in me than the world against me. Who can stand against me with you on my side? I cast my fear on you. I am no longer a slave to fear because I am your child. Help me to face my fears with the confidence that you've never lost a battle. Help me to walk in victory in Jesus' name. Amen.

<u>Personal Thoughts</u>

"Beethoven said that it's better to hit the wrong note confidently, than hit the right note unconfidently. Never be afraid to be wrong or to embarrass yourself; we are all students in this life, and there is always something more to learn."

Mike Norton

<u>**I've Got the Power**</u>

Today I'll remind you that God hasn't given us fear or anything resembling or resulting from it.

2 Tim. 1:7 (NLT) - *"God hasn't given us a spirit of fear and timidity but of power..."*

I Have the Power!

Perhaps you might be familiar with Masters of the Universe and its main character He-man, a cartoon figure from the 80's and 90's, who was this seemingly ordinary man living a run of the mill life. In times of distress and emergencies, he would draw out his sword and boldly declare, "I have the power!" After which, this ordinary man would miraculously be transformed into the strongest man in the universe. Everything about him instantly changed; from his common attire to his petrified cat. Everything was transformed. After this transformation, he had extraordinary strength, speed and even breath. His fearful feline became a fierce battle tiger. When transformed by the power, Heman was unstoppable.

Dare I say to you today, He-man was a fictional cartoon but you are the reality. You might seem weak and even feel like it but when transformed by the power of the Holy Spirit, you can say with confidence "I have the Power!" and the reality of that power would drive you to conquer any problem or situation. No wonder Jesus commanded His disciples to remain in Jerusalem till you are endued or clothed with power. He knew that this same power, which was equivalent to the power that raised Christ from the dead, would be necessary for the disciples to experience for their daily challenges in the faith.

God has invested power in you. Not the type to just turn your lights on or charge your cell phone, but the type of power that reaches the realities that you face every day. God has invested so much in you that He has afforded you the same power that Jesus had. Power over sickness; power over debt; power of demons; power over sin; power over every obstacle and opposition that you face. The next battle you face, pause for a minute and look at your situation and declare, "in the name of Jesus Christ, I have the Power" and go out and conquer your enemy in His name.

<u>Supplemental Scriptures:</u>

Acts 1:8	Acts 2	Zechariah 4:6
Luke 10:19	Micah 3:8	Luke 24:49

<u>Prayer</u>

Lord, thank you for power to conquer every foe whether physical, emotional, or spiritual. Thank you that I have the promise of the Holy Spirit as a Comforter and as the Giver of the power to win. Thank you for the power to serve you. Thank you for the power to forgive. Thank you for the power to love my enemies. Thank you for the power to be victorious. Help me walk and live in power. Thank you for the power to uphold your truth and be your witness. Help me to be wise and remain humble and responsible with my the victory that you give me in Jesus' name. Amen.

Personal Thoughts

"At any given moment you have the power to say this is
not how the story is going to end"

Anonymous

<u>**Dare 2 Love**</u>

Start today with the understanding that God hasn't given us fear but He has given us power and so much more.

1 Tim. 1:7 (NLT) - *"God has not given us a spirit of fear but of power, love..."*

Dare 2 Love

Love is such a hard subject to deal with because it has so many varying definitions and understandings that are often debated. The world and secular thought has clouded the subject of what true love really is. Soap operas thrived for decades and maybe more building their foundation on the discovery, maintenance, and overall melodrama of love. Unfortunately, there is so much misconception revolved around love in our entertainment that it is almost impossible to fully grasp the immensity of the subject.

The love often expressed in this society is superficial and selfish. Everyone seems to pursue love from a self-centered standpoint with little concern for the effects on others. This mentality forces one to put up high walls to protect themselves. There is nothing wrong with being guarded but a whole other thing to be trapped in a world without experiencing the wonders of real love; The type of love that invades your life both giving and taking in a synergy of mutual respect and gratification. Let's be honest for a moment and speak truth to power. Sometimes it's hard to love because of the fear of being hurt, betrayed, taken for granted, and/or short changed. But God has not imprisoned you to fear but through His love has released you to experience love and share it also.

Real love; God's love, brings freedom to you as you seek the good for others. One of the problems is that many people say it but don't do it. 1 John 3:18 says, "...*let's not just talk about love; let's practice real love*" (Message Bible). Real strength is not loving someone that you are fond of, but rather being an instrument of God's love to a stranger or even yet an enemy. Jesus commanded His disciples to love their enemies and to do good to them that did them harm. It is not easy but possible through Christ. To love is to imitate God.   God gives because of love; He saves because of love; He protects and provides because of love; Everything He does is because of love so what you've received from Him should be shared with someone else. It may sound corny until you're on the other end.

<u>Supplemental Scriptures:</u>

God is love	Galatians 5:14	Galatians 5:22
Colossians 1:8	1 Peter 1:22	Romans 5:5

<u>Prayer</u>

Lord, you designed me to love but I have experience so much hurt in my life that it's hard to love at times. You created me to imitate you with your expressions of love but life has left me wounded. I relive the scene of my pain so much that I can't imagine ever loving again but thank you for liberating me through your love. I am healed and can experience love again. As I give myself to you, let your love consume me and change my perspective towards others. Let my heart heal and help me to love again in Jesus' name. Amen.

Personal Thoughts

"In love, we have to dare everything if we really love"

Alain Delon

It's Time for a Beat Down

Grasp the reality that God hasn't given us fear but He has given us power and love.

2 Tim. 1:7 (NLT) - *"For God has not given us the spirit of fear, but of power, love and self-control."*

I vividly recall the experience of a very talented co-worker who would sadly forfeit many opportunities for growth and promotion simply because they couldn't possess self-control. They would constantly allow frustrations and the emotional roller coaster to continually stumble in their performance and behavior on the job. Ultimately, an opportunity for a promotion presented itself but they failed to obtain the position because the new projected supervisor didn't believe that they would be an asset because of their lack of discipline.   This got me thinking about the importance of self-control. Self-control seems to be unattainable for many people today. Yes, God has given us power, love, and self-control but the truth is too often many of us find ourselves like Paul; we do the things we don't really want to do and don't do the things that we know we ought to do. Let's not throw stones while living in glass houses. Let us look at ourselves first.

The Bible says in Proverbs 25:28 that we are like a defenseless city without self-control. We become vulnerable to any invasion of temptation and devilish persuasion. Yes, even as Christians.
 That's why for some of us, it doesn't take much for us to fly off the handle or be compulsive without thinking about the consequences. Ultimately, we end up losing God's intended blessing because we get out of control.

Paul has an easy answer for our problem. He says in 1 Cor. 9:27 that he buffets his body. What he is saying is that he lays the smackdown on his self, his flesh, his sexual proclivities, his anger, and the list can go on and on. Paul would train his body with self-control to accomplish greater things for God. For those who follow wrestling, the next time you get ready to curse, kick, scratch, gossip, etc... learn to pump your brakes and do an Undertaker tombstone on self. Create space for God to intervene with His grace which is sufficient to handle every situation in a God-honoring way.

Take these goods (power, love, and self-control) and conquer for Christ all your obstacles, setbacks and opposition as you possess your destiny.

<u>Supplemental Scriptures:</u>

Proverbs 25:28	Proverbs 16:32	2 Peter 1:5-7
Galatians 5:22-23	Proverbs 18:21	Titus 2:11-12

<u>Prayer</u>

Lord, I understand how the Apostle Paul felt as he desired to do good but ended up doing wrong. There have been moments that I have lost control over myself in situations and have let my anger and frustration get the best of me. Lord, I need self-control and it comes by submitting to your will so I surrender my will for yours. Give me grace to be under control in every circumstance. Help me experience the fruit of the Spirit that my life will be productive and others will see your work in my life in Jesus' name. Amen

Personal Thoughts

"If you learn self-control, you can master anything."

Anonymous

He Chose to Come to You

I can't fathom the feeling that people in the Bible must have felt to travel and see Jesus in the manger and how that experience must have changed their lives. The Bible brilliantly describes the wisemen who traveled from far through different terrains and threats just to see baby Jesus. The shepherds, who were not admired in that society, risked criticism and scrutiny just to go and see baby Jesus. Even the angels paused their Heavenly duties and formed a choir to serenade the baby King. Let's just be honest. No matter what our schedules looked like, we would have dropped everything and paid any price just to get a glimpse of the Savior of the world for a brief moment.

What's amazing about the story of a miraculously pregnant virgin who had a baby in a manager is that with all the fanfare that baby Jesus generated, His birth really wasn't the centerpiece of the story. The real gift wasn't His astonishing birth but more so that He chose to come for you and me. We didn't choose to be born or to what circumstance we were born in but Jesus chose to be born in a manger to poor parents with hay and the stench of animals just for an opportunity to eventually save you and me. He chose to come from eternity where there is no time, no aging, no pain, no sorrow, or death. He chose to enter into this life and existence to come close to us and bring us back to God Himself. He didn't choose an angel to do the work; He chose to come Himself. He didn't come as a dog, bird, or any other household pet, but He chose to come as a human baby that would eventually grow to become human sacrifice in order to take on the sin of the world and bring salvation.

I want you to consider that He wasn't forced by His Heavenly Father to come. He chose to come of His own volition knowing the consequences of loving us. He knew that we would disappoint Him, frustrate Him, betray Him and even deny Him, yet He chose to come anyway. Someone would say that it was reckless. Others would say that He was insane. It is amazing to me in spite of knowing all of the facts and all of our history, Jesus still chose to come for you and for me. The next time you start to celebrate your religiosity and believe that you are doing God a favor by showing up to a church service or performing some community service, remember that you didn't chose Him before He chose to come for you.

<u>Supplemental Scriptures:</u>

1 Peter 2:9	Ephesians 1:4-5	John 6:44
Romans 8:29-30	John 15:16	Deuteronomy 7:6

<u>Prayer</u>

Lord, where would I be without your grace and mercy? Thank you for choosing to be born so that you can die for my sins. Thank you for choosing me before I could choose you. Thank you for enduring the pain of sin by choice. You could have come in splendor but yet you chose a manager with the sheep and other animals just to have an opportunity to change my life. Thank you that you counted the cost and didn't consider me worthless but you thought I worth saving and keeping. You chose me so help me to in faith always choose you. Give the grace to see the value of having a relationship with you. May my response simply be yes. Help me to remember and cherish your choice as I live for you the rest of my days in Jesus' name. Amen.

Personal Thoughts

"Long before the enemy targeted you, God chose you"

Lisa Bevere

Day to Day

By the end of the first week of a new year, most aspirations have already been thrown in the garbage bin. It is so easy to make a new year's resolution before the ball drops and lose steam within the first few weeks of the new year. A New Year's resolution is a decision to either do or not do something to accomplish a personal goal of improvement as the new year begins. Some common New Year's resolutions are more exercise, less chocolate, a change of diet or some other alteration to an undesired behavior. There are some people who would attempt to convince you that it is pointless to make resolutions but I don't really buy into that school of thought.

Goals are important for success in life because setting goals is a vital ingredient in the planning process. I have heard all my life that if you fail to plan, you plan to fail. Eliminating goals from your life seems a bit drastic and shortsighted. Now, there is an argument for avoiding the pursuit of unrealistic goals and aspirations in a short space of time which would most likely lead to frustration and ultimate abandonment. Many resolutions die under the pressure of keeping up the pace. Let's make it even clearer. Many resolutions die under the pace of keeping up with people's opinion of your resolutions rather than your own convictions.

Instead of forming impractical grandiose resolutions that quickly die, it might make better sense to set goals and work at them day to day. This approach avoids trying to build Rome in a day but rather make progress moment by moment within the parameters of a day as they come. This is not spontaneously moving through each day with a Que Sera, Sera mentality. Day to day sounds so slow but it is effective. Mignon McLaughlin says, "The only courage that matters is the kind that gets you from one moment to the next." We have been all blessed to have 24 hours in a day and the responsibility to achieve fulfillment in those moments. When we attempt to live in the future with its possibilities, we risk missing the enjoyment of the right now moment. Am I saying to forget about setting resolutions? No. I am prescribing an approach that views the day to day moments as the perfect canvas to build your life in. Day to day becomes weeks; then months; then years; then a lifetime. It all starts in the precious moments of the day to day. Start with the first step and then build your marathon journey.

<u>Supplemental Scriptures:</u>

Matthew 6:11	Psalm 118:24	1 Kings 8:66
Isaiah 40:31	Proverbs 3:5-6	Exodus 20:11

<u>Prayer</u>

Lord, you taught your disciples to request daily bread. You've always desired us to depend on you. Thank you that I don't have to stress and worry but hold your hands day by day. Thank you that you give me 24 hours in a day to love and forgive. Thank you that you are with me in every moment so every moment becomes like heaven. Lord, help me to maximize my time and completely trust you to guide me through each day. Help me to draw close to you and be content with your provision. Help me not to become greedy or wasteful but use each day to do your will and enjoy your presence in Jesus' name. Amen

Personal Thoughts

"People often say that motivation doesn't last. Well,
neither does bathing that's why we recommend it daily."

Zig Ziglar

Can't You See It?

I recently attended a fundraiser concert for a mission's venture in South Africa. I arrived late and the concert had already started and I was stuck in the back of the sanctuary because there were limited seats. It was dark and crowded and the only seat I could find was behind a pillar with limited view of the stage. For a while I settled for just being in the building and hearing the great music from all of the artists. I truly wasn't comfortable with my seating but it was my only option.

Suddenly I saw a friend of mine who happened to be a guest artist on the program. After greeting each other, she asked me why I was sitting so far back. She proceeded to check for seating closer to the stage with better view. After checking, she texted me about some available seating closer to the platform with a phenomenal view. As I read her text about the better seating, I was reluctant to leave my seat because I couldn't see where she was directing me. All I had to go on was her viewpoint and her word. I almost stayed where I was because it was easier to stay where I was than to take a risk for seating that I couldn't see. My seating gave me limited delight and I was willing to remain limited to avoid risking my comfort.

In that moment I realized that God is constantly attempting to redirect us so that we are able to maximize every experience. God always gives us insight to superior levels of existence and operation from a greater viewpoint than us. He is omniscient; He knows all things. We have to trust His word and wisdom even when we can't see the end result. Someone says, "We should trust

God even when we can't trace Him." I eventually moved out on my friend's advice and surely there was empty seats closer to the action. My new seat gave me an up-close vantage point where I could hear, see, and interact with the flow of the concert with greater enjoyment. If we would move in sync with God's word and His flow, we would have greater experiences with Him and maximize every opportunity in life. Our life would be lived on a greater level. So, we have to trust Him and believe that He:

1. Is concerned about where we are
2. Can see what's ahead.
3. Won't give us bad or unfavorable advice and won't pilot us erroneously.

Trust Him today with all your concerns and follow His advice. You'll enjoy the results.

Supplemental Scriptures:

Proverbs 3:5-6	Proverbs 22:19	Job 13:15
Psalm 37:3-7	Psalm 62:8	Psalm 115:9

Prayer

Lord, there are many times that I miss what you are doing in my life because I can't see it. There are so many times that you are working on my behalf and revealing marvelous things about where you are taking me but I hesitate because I can't discern it. Help me to trust you when I can't trace you. Help me to lean on you even when I don't understand you or your ways. Help me to rest in your promise, your resume, and your plan for me. Open my eyes that I may see you always at work in Jesus' name. Amen.

<u>Personal Thoughts</u>

"God does not guide those who want to run their own life"

Winkie Pratney

Foot Prints in the Sand

I have been a Junior my whole life. I've grown up in the shadow of a great father and have enjoyed carrying his precious name my entire life. He has taught me a lot about life, God, and just being a man. He has set the standard high with great tangible examples of manhood for me to follow. You can say that he left me big foot prints to trail. This is great for any son looking up to their dad and receiving the gift of mentorship.

There is a popular and inspirational poem written by an anonymous author entitled "Foot prints in the sand". The story revolves about a man who dreamed of walking on the beach with God. At a certain point, he saw two foot prints signifying that God was with him. It is a great feeling to know that God is with you through your ups and downs. David said. "Yea, though I walk through the valley of the shadow of death, I will fear no evil: for thou are with me…" The poem further describes that the man then saw only one set of prints. I'm sure he thought to himself, "Where is God?" Have you ever felt that way?

The revelation of the singular foot prints didn't expose that God had abandoned him but rather that God had carried him. The foot prints weren't his lonely foot prints trying to survive on his own. Those foot prints were God's foot prints carrying him through his ordeal. How many times have you seen the singular foot prints and assumed that you were alone? Could it be that God was actually carrying you through your circumstances this whole time? You weren't operating under your own strength but the strength of God. His grace does way more for us than we give Him credit for.

I encourage you to pause and think about how many times that He has carried you through the difficulties and challenges of your life. For some, you can easily reflect those precious moments of feeling His support, and, for others, you are now realizing that He is actually carrying you through something right now.

It's wonderful to consider that God never gets tired of carrying us over obstacles and the rough patches of our lives. There is no situation that He won't be there for us. He's never too busy to invade our situation, pick us up, and carry us. You are going to make it because you don't have to get over it. Just embrace His love and grace and let Him carry you.

<u>Supplemental Scriptures</u>:
Isaiah 46:4   Isaiah 47:1-15   Isaiah 44:2
Exodus 15:11   Isaiah 43:13   Psalm 92:14

<u>Prayer</u>

Lord, I want to thank you for always being there for me especially when I don't acknowledge you. There are times that I just complain and complain instead of realizing that you have always looked out for me. There are times when I doubt you and then feel foolish when you come through in a marvelous way. Lord, help me to recognize that its by your strength that I have overcome my obstacles. Help me to recognize that my victory comes from you and not my education; not my network; not my gift or personality. Thank you for carrying me. Help me to witness to others about your mighty acts and testify of your greatness in Jesus' name. Amen

Personal Thoughts

"Wherever you go, whatever you do, I'll always be there supporting you"

Anonymous

The FORCE be with you

I am a science fiction geek. Yes, I admit it. It is true. So with that said, you must understand that movies like Star Trek and Star Wars are always at the top of the list. Don't ask me to choose between these two in particular. I will always choose both or plead the fifth. But within the Star Wars' saga, there were an ancient order of protectors united by their ability to harness the power of the FORCE. These galactic leaders and peace keepers were guardians of truth and justice and embarked on a great task of maintaining order throughout the universe. They fought against the evils of the dark side and those within their universe that pursued dominance and unbridled power. The Jedi relied heavily on their connection to each other and the FORCE within them to accomplish their missions.

The FORCE in this world is described as the power of Cosmos; an energy field created by all living things. It surrounds and penetrates them while binding the galaxy together. Jedi believed that the FORCE was beyond their understanding. There was a light and dark side in constant opposition. The light sought emphasized compassion and courage while avoiding unbridled passion and corruption. The force was a benefit to the Jedi and you often here, "May the FORCE be with you." This was to wish that the FORCE would work favorable for the person.

As believers, we hold to the truth that we have been afforded dynamic help in this Christian journey. Jesus commanded his disciples to wait in Jerusalem to be endued with power. The power that He spoke of would enable a believer to accomplish the will of God and mission of God for their life. This power was necessary for success just like the FORCE in Star Wars. The biggest difference is that the power that Jesus spoke of was not a FORCE but the consequence of connecting with the Holy Spirit. The Holy Spirit was promised from God to help us get through the various issues and struggles of being a Christian. He's not a FORCE but the third person of the Trinity and He releases power, comfort, guidance, and so much more in our lives. In Star Wars it was appropriate for the Jedi to pronounce the blessing and favor of the FORCE but in reality, believers seek the power and presence of the Holy Spirit to enable our success in ministry, marriage, and life in general. So, the next time you leave a believer's presence, say this, "May the Spirit be with you". I know that it sounds too deep or really corny but think about it. What more could we ask for but to have the Holy Spirit's assistance in all our endeavors. Let me impart this in your day today. "May the Spirit be with you."

Supplemental Scriptures:

| Acts 1:8 | Psalm 32:8 | Joel 2 |
| Acts 2:4 | Acts 6:8 | Micah 3:8 |

Prayer

Lord thank you for connecting me to a bigger purpose than I can imagine. Thank you for giving me your Spirt guide, protect, and bless my life. It's in you that I can face giants; It's in you that I can speak to my challenges and see change. It's in you that I can win every battle and outlast every war. Thank you for your Spirit in me that I am more than a conqueror. Help me to be disciplined and never forget that my greatest victories come from my connection to purpose and your will for my life. I pray that you will help me be blessing to others wherever I go and the favor of God go before me; let goodness and mercy follow me; let your presence live inside me in Jesus' name. Amen.

Personal Thoughts

"When we have the Holy Spirit, we have all that is
needed to be all that God desires us to be"

Aiden Wilson Tozer

References

Angelou, M. (1969) *I Know Why the Cage Bird Sings*. New York. Random House LLC.

Emerson, R. (1994) *Collected Poems and Translations*. New York. Penguin Putnam Inc.

Footprints in the Sand. [circa, 1922]

Goodrich, R. (2015*) Smile Anyway: Quotes, Verse, and Grumblings of Everyday of the Year*. Create Space Independent Publishing Platform.

McFadden, Gene, Cohen, Jerry and Whitehead, John. (1978) Aint No Stoppin' Us Now [Recorded by Nylons] on McFadden & Whitehead. Philadelphia International. Accessed online https://www.warnerchappell.com/song-details/WW%20001083227%2000/84c472f9-bdbb-41d4-ae97-bdb4ea1c2655

Westfal, W. (2013) *Dream Operative*. Westfal Publishing & Graphics LLC.

About the Author

Stanford Senior, Jr. is communicator of God's truth through diverse means. He is a young adult pastor at Mt. Bethel Church of God in Trenton, NJ and a graduate of Lee university in Cleveland, TN with a Bachelors of Science in Christian Ministry and a Masters of Arts in Ministry Leadership. He has always loved writing and sharing complex gospel truths in simplistic ways that make God and His Kingdom easy to grasp. He has had the great opportunity to share God's word and truth in various settings including revivals, conferences, seminars, and workshops both in the United States and Internationally. His love and desire is to help people see what God sees when He looks at us and share God's heart and purpose for people.